Poems of Faith to Challenge, to Encourage, and to Inspire

Poems of Faith to Challenge, to Encourage, and to Inspire

Gary S Mathis

gatekeeper press™

Columbus, Ohio

Poems of Faith to Challenge, to Encourage, and to Inspire

Published by Gatekeeper Press
2167 Stringtown Rd, Suite 109
Columbus, OH 43123-2989
www.GatekeeperPress.com

Library of Congress Control Number: 2022937592

ISBN (paperback): 9781662927065

Dedication

This book is dedicated to and in memory of
my wonderful and loving mother
who loved poems of faith and inspiration
but who loved me so much more.
Two poems in this book
were written in her honor.

Special thanks given to Shirley Branson, Carolyn Tilley, and
the ladies of the Kingston City Library.

Contents

The Story Behind the Poems

As you read these poems, I must tell you the story about the amazing experience that led up to this book of poems: A miraculous three-day period in which the Holy Spirit granted me the ability to do something I had "never" been able to do before.

You should know that I am a sixty-six-year-old retired math teacher, who knew from the beginning, that the Lord had "called" me to be a teacher. I enjoyed thirty-seven wonderful years of being used by the Lord to touch the hearts and minds of students. After I retired, I began praying about what plan or purpose the Lord had for me now. I had always enjoyed music and singing in a choir, but to write a poem or a song was practically impossible. I excelled in math, but the subject of English was, by far, my most difficult subject. I don't ever remember writing an acceptable poem, and to write one at my age and being so poetically challenged seemed like a waste of time. But despite this, my desire was to write a song. Since I realized most songs were poems set to music, I knew God would have to do a true miracle for me to write one.

After the Covid 19 outbreak, I began memorizing countless verses of scripture every week, and read more than one hundred Christian books. Without realizing it, God had been filling me with passion and inspiration which seemed to "explode" out of me when I attempted to write my first poem.

So, on Tuesday, November 16, 2021, I decided I would pray to the Lord to ask Him to allow me to write just "one" song. After praying, I began to write knowing that I had nothing to lose. Little did I know, the Lord had a much greater purpose to reveal to me than to write a song. So, as I began to write, thoughts came to me from the depths of my soul. I let the Holy Spirit guide my feelings and show me the words to use as I wrote. Surprisingly, in a very short time, I had written my first ever poem: "The One I Will Live For." I was stunned when I read the poem. True, it would need revision and more time later to edit, but it sounded better than I had anticipated. But the ideas didn't stop there.

They began to flood out of my heart, and before I knew it, the Holy Spirit had quickly given me another poem. To my amazement, He then gave me a third, and a fourth, and finally a fifth. I had only been writing for a part of a day, and the Lord had given me five poems. It was like a dream, and it didn't seem real.

The next day the Lord gave me many more ideas, so I continued to write more poems. Now, my desire was to no longer just write a song, but to write any and every poem the Holy Spirit might impart to me. Miraculously, the Holy Spirit inspired me to write eight more poems before the day ended. Thoughts and ideas came so fast, I had never experienced anything like this before. I remember trying to fix dinner and having to stop several times so I could go to the other room to write down the thoughts before I forgot them. Finally, I knew I had to finish fixing the meal. But, as I sat down to eat, I had to run to the other room to write down more thoughts. A similar thing happened that night when I had to get up a few times to write down thoughts so as not to forget.

On Thursday, November 18th, I could not stop writing. I didn't attempt to figure out what was going on, but just kept writing. Astonishingly, the Lord gave me eight more poems on Thursday for a total of twenty-one. Friday, I stopped writing, and began to read the poems the Holy Spirit had given me. I was stunned and speechless. I knew these poems had not come from my ability or wisdom. I wasn't capable of writing all of these poems, much less in a three-day period. Since these poems were from the Holy Spirit, I asked the Lord what He would have me do with them. The Lord had already accomplished through me far more than I dreamed was possible and had originally purposed to do. I wondered if other people would feel the same way about these poems as I felt.

After spending time on Friday and Saturday editing and making corrections the best I knew how, on Sunday morning I felt led to text my minister of Music. I told him I had something for him to read that morning before the Thanksgiving service. My fourteenth poem had been written as a Thanksgiving poem entitled, "I Thank Him For." At church that morning after reading the poem, he asked me if he could read this poem to the congregation just before the last song before the message. I asked him just to say a member of the congregation had written it. I was amazed how the Lord orchestrated the events that morning. Every song we sang was brought out in this poem. Later that day, I attempted to write another poem. But instead of allowing the Holy Spirit to guide me as before, I began to write a poem in my own wisdom and power. It was a failure. The Holy Spirit taught me a valuable lesson. If I were to continue to write poems, I must totally rely on the Spirit to direct me when and how to write them. I spent the next two days editing

Monday evening, I prayed for the Lord to give me a tune for one of my poems. I knew if He did that, it would be as great a miracle as it had been for me to write poetry. It was a selfish request, but graciously that night, God gave me a tune for my tenth poem: "Give It to Jesus." Tuesday morning, November 23rd, I awoke and was surprised to remember the tune. As the days went on, I tried to keep the tune in my head. Soon after that the Lord gave me a tune for another poem, which I would continually sing so as not to forget the melody. Unbelievably the Lord had given me two songs. Even though the Lord had answered my prayer, I realized His main priority was for me to write poems given by the Holy Spirit that might challenge, encourage, inspire, motivate, or convict others.

Tuesday afternoon I called a very dear friend whom I check on often and who was a close friend to my mother. I consider her like a second mother, and one who had written poems herself earlier in her life. As we talked, I happened to mention what the Lord had been doing for me, knowing it would make her happy. She asked me to read a poem for her, but after hearing one poem, she wanted to hear more. I could tell how much she enjoyed hearing them, and how meaningful and inspirational they were to her. She immediately encouraged me to get them published, and that it would encourage and inspire many others. If this was the Lord's will for me to have these poems published, we both would pray for the Holy Spirit to guide and direct me to the right publisher. She recommended I write the story behind the writing of these poems after hearing me share some of the story with her. In the next several days, the Lord gave me twenty-three more poems. I now had forty-four poems and decided this would be enough for a possible publication. The Lord had different plans. A few days later, He inspired me to write five more, and one would become a favorite. This poem happened to be my forty-ninth poem, "The Best Gift," and was based on a true story. Soon after that He gave me nineteen more. Twelve of these also became favorites. I eventually would select the top fifty-five and completely trust God to show me how to proceed.

Even though I started out wanting to write a song, the Lord revealed to me a much greater purpose. I desire that these poems be used for His will, for His glory, and for His purpose. I hope the poems will get into the hands of people that might be helped. Though these poems are very simplistic and don't possess the experience of a seasoned and gifted poet, I feel they can inspire and encourage many who will read them. I sincerely hope that unbelievers will read them and will be interested to find out about this Savior, Who can give them a love, joy, hope, and peace they have never experienced. They may realize just how much God loves them and has a plan and purpose for their lives. They may also see that Jesus came to this earth to die for us and our sins and provide the only way to receive an abundant life here on this earth, and an eternal life with Him in heaven after this life. Hopefully they will realize Christianity is a personal intimate relationship with God Himself, and that God can be known. Since these poems are His, I shall place them in His hands for Him to use as He chooses. May God touch your heart and bless your soul as these poems have touched and blessed me.

Author's Note

References have been placed above some of the poems in this book and are scripture verses, which were referred to in the poem itself.

The Inspiration Behind the Poems

My desire to write these poems
    was to challenge, encourage, and inspire.
I hoped my readers would find,
    whatever, they needed or desired to acquire.
My readers might find renewed strength and encouragement
    to deal with the challenges they face.
Some might be reminded and reassured
    of God's great love, mercy, and grace.
Some might find a poem,
    to which they could personally relate:
Words which have a special meaning
    and seem written just for their sake.
Some might be challenged and motivated
    to try things previously thought impossible.
And after reading the story behind the poems,
    might give them hope that anything is possible.
Some people might be given renewed hope and joy
    that will carry them through another day.
To direct their hearts and thoughts to Christ
    is what I desire and do pray.
Some might be led to salvation through Jesus,
    and this is worth more than anything on this earth;
What joy it is to receive eternal life
    and experience a miraculous new birth.
You can't imagine what joy
    God has brought to my heart.
To write down these poems
    the Holy Spirit did truly impart.

My Mom

My mom loved me more
    than any mom could love a son.
She was so proud of me
    that to her, I was "second" to none.
She enjoyed doing things for me
    and was always there when needed.
She was ready to encourage or uplift me
    whenever I felt defeated.
We enjoyed going places together
    and saw many wonderful sites.
Traveling places with me
    was for her such great delight.
We enjoyed Christian concerts
    and the many uplifting songs to hear.
Music was such a joy for us,
    and it gave us so much cheer.
My mom absolutely loved planting flowers
    and watching them grow.
She could tell me about every flower,
    which I might want to know.
My mom would spend hours in her backyard
    admiring God's beauty.
Colorful bushes, trees, and flowers
    all captured her attention fully.
My mom was ever joyful,
    and she always had a smile to share.
She had such a heart for others,
    and others knew she cared.
My mom would always try to encourage
    those who might be down.
She was a person when others met her,
    they wanted to be around.

My mom loved to laugh
    and enjoyed being with her friends.
She was so grateful for all the blessings,
    which God did graciously send.
My mom loved the Lord
    and wanted others to know about Christ.
Even nearing death, Mom shared with an aide
    about Him who gives life.
My mom also enjoyed reading poems,
    especially inspiring ones she might find.
I can only imagine how she would have felt
    reading these poems of mine.
You may not have had a mother
    who showed much love for you.
But you do have a Father in heaven
    who truly loves you, even more, too!

Just Like Me

The little boy had just recently been adopted; that
    had been no easy task.
Only having one leg and a slightly deformed body
    had hindered him being adopted in the past.
He now had Godly parents,
    and they were taking him to get a puppy.
He was so excited about this trip
    and felt so very lucky.
They arrived at the animal shelter,
    and with his crutches he hopped inside.
He carefully looked at each dog
    trying to find just the right prize.
Each dog barked eagerly at him
    and wagged their tails about.
But the boy had yet to see the one
    that he would hopefully take out.
He then came to a cage
    where the dog just lay sadly at the back.
It just slowly raised its head
    and then laid it back down on the mat.
The boy asked to go inside
    feeling much compassion for this dog.
Just as the boy had once felt,
    the dog seemed to feel he didn't belong.
As the boy got closer to the dog,
    the puppy slowly staggered to stand up.
You see, the dog was missing a leg too
    and was a slightly deformed pup.
The boy fell in love with this puppy
    because they were so much alike.
The puppy wanted him too,
    and it gave the boy overwhelming delight.

The boy took the dog home,
   and they became inseparable friends.
They both found a companion
   that unconditionally loved each other to the end.
Aren't you glad that God loves us
   in the same way too?
Let's pray that God will use us to show
   His unconditional love through.

There Is No

There is no trial we will face
    that our Heavenly Father does not know.
Though, He wants to use the trial
    so that we might surely grow.
The trials will help us grow spiritually
    and help our faith to become strong.
Even through these trials,
    we can still sing a joyous song.
There is no problem we will face
    that our Heavenly Father cannot solve.
But He wants us to trust Him
    for all that it might involve.
He wants us to find the answer with His help,
    and not by us alone.
Then the problem can be solved
    and finally it will be all gone.
There is no mountain of challenge we will face
    that is too high for us to scale.
If we rely on God,
    we surely cannot fail.
Though it may seem impossible
    to ever overcome,
we'll find through God's power
    it truly can be done.
There is no sin we will face
    that is too great to defeat.
If we confess, repent, and forsake it,
    then it can be beat.
Our God will forgive our sins
    through His obedient Son
who by His blood on Calvary's cross
    said, "It-Is-Finished" and thus we know it's done!

When We Suffer Hardship

When difficulties and trials come,
    we usually pray for immediate relief.
Though the opposite should be true,
    and not see difficulties as just a grief.
Instead, we must see them as a way
    to spiritually grow and mature.
For if we lived without trials, we would grow
    too uncaring, proud, and self-assured.
When we suffer hardship, we have more compassion
    for those who suffer the same.
When we suffer hardship, we can feel more empathy
    for others facing pain.
When we suffer hardship, we find ourselves
    developing greater faith and humility.
When we suffer hardship, we find how weak
    and limited we are in our own ability.
When we suffer hardship, we must learn
    to be totally dependent on Christ.
When we suffer hardship, we learn that
    only Christ's strength and power will suffice.
When we suffer hardship, we discover
    we grow much closer to the Lord.
When we suffer hardship, we find we appreciate
    Christ's love so much more.
Therefore, when weighing the pros and cons of trials,
    the benefits cannot be compared.
The more a person is spiritually mature
    the greater the crosses he's had to bear.
So, we must allow these difficulties
    to mold us into what God wants us to be.
And pray that God will give us
    the strength and perseverance that we will need.

I Saw a Man

I saw a man
    whom I did not know.
He seemed lost
    not knowing where to go.
I asked him if
    I could help him some way.
He wanted to know
    if for him I might pray.
He wanted to find his purpose
    and meaning in life.
He wanted to be eased
    of his toil and his strife.
I gladly agreed
    to pray for His needs
Hoping I might sow
    some precious seeds.
I wanted to lead him to seek
    for the one who can save,
God's only Son, Jesus Christ
    who out of His love He gave.
As I prayed for the man,
    he sobbed and became convicted.
The Holy Spirit began His work
    as I might have predicted.
Suddenly all the man's problems
    vanished far away.
He had found Jesus
    and His awesome love that day.
Now, the man is my brother
    in Christ, don't you see.
His life is now changed,
    and the Lord has "somewhat" changed me.

The Rapture
(1 Thess. 4:16-17; Matt. 24:36-44; Mark 13:32-37)

A man was driving home with his wife
   when his wife suddenly disappeared.
The man took a double take and then he began
   to experience shock and fear.
Driverless cars began to crash all around him
   and he couldn't just pretend
what he saw did not really happen,
   but that it was just impossible to comprehend.
He turned on the radio to discover
   thousands of people could not be found.
Especially all the children in nurseries
   and preschools that were no longer around.
Fires, explosions, and accidents were occurring
   because missing key workers couldn't do their tasks.
He stopped at a store to find out what was happening
   and to find someone he could ask.
No one could tell him what was happening
   and everyone had panic and fear.
Adults were missing children, spouses,
   and someone who was dear.
The strangest thing about this occurrence was that
   the valuables and clothes of missing people had been left.
The man suddenly remembered his wife's warning
   and what she believed and did accept.
She had told him Jesus was going to come back
   to rapture those who had believed.
Many would be left behind because they refused Christ
   and His salvation and forgiveness to receive.
The Bible had warned that the Rapture
   could occur at any time.
Please don't be like this man, but believe
   and receive Christ and don't be left behind.

Jesus: The Way, the Truth, and the Life
(John 14:1-10)

Jesus once said you believe in God,
    believe also in me.
In my Father's House are many mansions,
    and one day you will see.
I go to prepare a place for you
    and will come back one day.
I will receive you to myself
    where you will forever stay.
Where I go you will go too,
    and I will let you know.
I will show you the way
    and where I'm soon to go.
Thomas said, "How can we know
    where you're going to?"
Jesus said, "I AM the way"
    which shall also be for you.
Jesus also said, "I AM the truth"
    that will guide you as you go.
This is not something the world gives,
    but I give so my wisdom you will know.
Jesus said, "I AM the life"
    which I will give to you abundantly;
A life so full and so complete
    to be lived by you eternally.
No man comes to the Father
    except it be through me.
For you to enter the gates of heaven,
    I'm the one who has the key.
If you had known me,
    you should have known My Father also.

From now on you know Him,
    and have seen Him here below.
Phillip said, "Show us the Father,
    and it will be sufficient for us?"
Jesus said if you've seen me,
    you've seen the Father, which is enough.
Do, you believe I'm in the Father,
    and the Father is in me?
The words I speak are not my own,
    but by My Father's authority.
My Father dwells in me,
    and the works you see me do,
they can only be done in thee
    if you let me dwell in you.
So, trust completely in the Father
    abiding in Him who is above.
Then He will work through you
    accomplishing great things through His love.

Every Knee Shall Bow
(Phil 2:8-11)

Jesus Christ, God's Son, was once found
    in the appearance of a man.
He then humbled Himself
    and became obedient as any man can.

He was obedient to the point of death,
    and even the death on a cruel Roman cross.
His death to His disciples, friends, and family
    was an insurmountable loss.

But God the Father highly exalted Him
    and gave His Son a wonderful name.
He gave Him a name above all others,
    and one that would be of everlasting fame.

That at the name of Jesus
    every knee on earth will bow.
Those which are in heaven,
    and those under the earth also shall.

They will also confess with their mouth
    that Jesus Christ is "Lord."
Confessing to the glory of God the father
    that He is the Lord of Lords to be adored.

Give It to Jesus

(First Ever Song with Tune)
(A Song or Hymn)

Are you searching to find some meaning in your life?
    Are you hoping there's something to ease all your strife?
Are you seeking a way to bring you some hope?
    Are you praying you will find the strength to cope?

The answer is not far and is easy to discover.
    Jesus *Is* the answer, and there *Is* no other.
He can meet every need and every problem you face.
    So, give it to Jesus to run well life's race.

Just give it to Jesus to run well life's race.
    Just give it to Jesus for no other can replace.
Just give it to Jesus, and you'll be eternally safe.
    Just give it to Jesus and keep seeking His face.

Now, you're searching for God's will to discover.
    Now, you're hoping for God's truth to uncover.
Now, you're seeking for God's presence all the time.
    Now, you're praying for God's love so divine.

The answer *was* not far and was "easy" to discover.
    Jesus *was* the answer, and there *was* no other.
He's met every need and every problem you'll face.
    You *gave* it to *Jesus* to run well life's race.

You *gave* it to *Jesus* to run well life's race.
    You *gave* it to *Jesus* and no other will replace.
You *gave* it to *Jesus* and you're now eternally safe.
    You *gave* it to *Jesus*, and there's nothing you can't face!

Complain! Complain!
(Eph. 5:20; Philippians 4:11; 1 Thess. 5:16, 18; Hebrews 13:5)

Complain! Complain! You say
    from your spouse complaining is all you hear?
And when they complain,
    all you can say is, "You are *so* right dear."
It's too hot or it's too cold!
    Some are never satisfied, and that's a fact.
So you tell them,
    "Honey, please just go and change the thermostat."
They say, "But you NEVER listen!
    I TRIED to tell you!"
Or maybe, "If ONLY you had DONE it,
    when I TOLD you to!"
How about, "But we've NEVER done it,
    that way before"?
Or even, "Can't you do
    ANYTHING right anymore?"
Complaining is never helpful
    in any way or in any situation.
All it does is cause others to avoid you
    and creates frustration.
There are many who never seem
    to be able to be content.
There is always something
    they want to complain about or resent.
God's Word tells us
    always to be thankful, and "in all things."
We are to be grateful and contented
    no matter what life brings.
If we will just learn
    that living this life is *not* all about us;
Therefore, it's important not to complain,
    but just learn "to adjust."

Train Up a Child
(Proverbs 22:6)

The young Christian couple sat proudly
   as they held their new baby boy.
The baby stared at them with wonder
   as they smiled at him with joy.
The parents had been changed forever
   by this precious gift from the Lord.
They thanked God for this beautiful, healthy baby,
   and they couldn't have loved him any more.
They now would have the responsibility
   to raise this child as Jesus would desire.
They would teach him to love the Lord
   and to learn to obey what He required.
They would dedicate and commit
   the life of this little boy to Christ.
They prayed that one day he would receive
   the gift of salvation and eternal life.
They would train him to read the Bible
   and to believe that it's God's Word.
They would train him to pray to God,
   and know that his prayers were being heard.
They would strive to be godly examples
   that their child could gladly follow.
They would teach him how much God loved him,
   Therefore, he need not worry about each tomorrow.
They would teach him that God alone
   was worthy of his worship and praise.
They would teach him to trust God completely
   for the rest of his remaining days.
The Bible tells us we are to train up a child
   in the way he should go.
And if we do, he will not depart from it
   when later in life he is old.

Live This Day as If Your Last
(Psalm 145:16; Ephesians 5:16)

I awoke today
    and gave thanks and praise
to be alive and to be
    given another day.
I wondered what this day
    might soon unfold;
Much uncertainty
    if the truth really be told.
But I know
    God is in control of all things.
Therefore, it really doesn't matter
    what this day may bring.
I also know
    God holds our future in His hands.
His future includes me
    whom He has in His eternal plans.
God's word tells us
    that we must redeem the time.
We must make the most
    of every opportunity that we find.
So, each morning when we rise
    we need to pray.
We need to ask God to help us
    make the most of that day.
What opportunities
    might this day bring forth?
It is exciting
    what our Father might have in store.
We must live this day
    as if it's our last,
living it usefully and wisely
    before it's past.

I Thank Him For

How can I say thanks to my Father in heaven above,
    who gives us all things because of His great love?
I thank Him for saving me from sin's wage
    through Christ's blood, the payment that He made.
I thank Him for my strength and good health,
    that is more valuable than all the earth's wealth.
I thank Him for giving me an earthly home
    and also one in heaven that later he'll make known.

I thank Him for a church in which to serve Him in.
    I'm able to serve with other believers and dear friends.
I thank Him for His many blessings which He gives.
    I want to praise Him for as long as I live.
I thank Him for His presence each day,
    and I long for that feeling "never" to go away.
I thank Him for His promise to never leave.
    Oh how much it comforts my fears to relieve.

I thank Him for His mercy and for His grace.
    It is like sweet honey which satisfies my taste.
I thank Him for His love that I joyfully feel.
    Oh how much I know that it's "so" real.
I thank Him for adopting me as His son,
    and what He desires for me to become.
I thank Him especially for the gift of eternal life.
    Oh how precious I must be in His sight.

How can I say thanks when not enough words can be said?
    There must be something which I can do instead.
Since words are not enough for all he has done,
    "My Life" must show the thanks when words cannot come.

The One I Have Been Waiting For
(Revelation 19: 7, 9)

The bride was so beautiful
  as she walked slowly down the aisle.
She arrived and stood next to her betrothed
  and flashed a radiant smile.
The groom lovingly looked at her
  and gave her a smile too.
It was a marriage made in heaven,
  And they couldn't wait to say, "I Do."
Each of them had something special to say
  as they stood together in one accord.
The bride told her beloved,
  "You are the one I have been waiting for."
The groom said, "You are worth more
  than the most costly pearl,
and I love you more
  than any one guy could love a girl."
The Bible speaks of the redeemed
  as the bride of Christ.
And one day Christ will come
  and take His redeemed to be His wife.
Actually this marriage was really made in heaven
  before life began;
For Christ to come to gather His elect
  was always God's eternal plan.
Yes, there is going to be a marriage supper
  with Christ, the great "I Am."
"Blessed are those who are called
  to the marriage supper of the Lamb."
This Marriage of the Lamb is coming,
  and His wife will be all prepared.
It's Christ Who's *The One* we will be waiting for,
  and no other will compare.

Christ Is Risen Indeed

(Matthew 28:12-15; Luke 24:6-7; John 20:13)

Jesus, the Lord and Savior,
    died on an old rugged cross.
Hopes and dreams of those who followed
    all seemed lost.
They saw Him buried
    and His tomb made very secure.
The one they hoped to be king
    seemed now so obscure.
But on that Easter morning
    the tomb was found vacant.
What could have happened?
    Where was our Lord taken?
The answer would soon be given
    that angels would proclaim.
"Christ has risen!" "He's risen indeed!"
    The sound of good news joyfully rang.
Our bless-ed Lord was alive.
    Jesus was really alive.
"It's not true," said the disbelievers,
    "This message has been contrived."
But Jesus appeared, to many,
    to show that it was true.
They all praised God
    for the joyful and wonderful, good news.
Rejoice! Rejoice!
    Let all that hath breath give God praise.
Jesus our Christ and Lord
    has from the dead been raised.
Now He reigns on high
    and is *Glorified* and *Exalted* for evermore.
Only Jesus Christ our Savior
    is worthy to live and die for.

The Wise Grandmother

A young boy was playing with a ball
    in his grandmother's front yard.
His mamaw was sitting in a chair
    knitting and not far.
A little neighbor girl came up to ask him
    if she could play with his ball.
The boy selfishly said no and told her
    just go away and play with her dolls.
She begged him once more, but he again
    refused to give his ball for her to play.
The girl began crying
    because of the unkind words the boy did say.
The grandmother had been watching
    all that had been going on.
She wisely had a plan that would teach a lesson
    and would right a wrong.
So instead of correcting her grandson
    for his very selfish action,
she pulled out a solid round object
    and began knitting over it with satisfaction.
Very expertly and quickly
    she began to knit round and round.
In a few minutes she had knitted a ball
    better than any could be found.
The boy watched with his mouth wide open
    and was absolutely stunned.
He could not believe
    what his grandmother had so amazingly done.
She gave the little girl the ball
    and told her that it was her very own.
The little girl joyfully took the ball
    and went away happily to her home.

The boy felt so bad
    and was even jealous of the girl's new ball.
The ball his mamaw had made
    was a much better ball than them all.
He didn't dare ask his mamaw
    for her to make him one too.
He realized how selfish he had been
    and his guilty action he couldn't undo.
The boy never forgot this lesson
    that his grandmother had taught.
Even years later he appreciated her godly wisdom
    that she had wisely brought.
You might ask, how do I know
    that this story is really true?
You see, I was that boy
    for whom this lesson was directed to.

So, You Think You Are Old?
(Psalm 37:25)

You once were young
    but now you're old.
O where, O where,
    does the time go?
You say that you don't
    have that much time left.
Every day has opportunities
    to be used for God Himself.
Yes, every day there is something
    worthwhile for you to do,
because God can and will
    do anything through you.
But you must pray to God that He
    will show you His plan and His will.
He will show you the plan He has for you now,
    and how He will use your life still.
God will reveal the ministries
    and opportunities that are just for you.
If you will just listen and be obedient
    to what God would have you do.
Then with God's help
    you can accomplish a great deal.
Though it will not be possible
    outside God's perfect will.
If God will use
    such an incompetent one like me,
God will without doubt
    use you most certainly.
These poems you are reading
    would never have come to be
if I hadn't trusted and believed the Lord
    would possibly use me.

You Can Have Joy Even When

You can have joy
    even when washing the dishes.
It may not be something
    that fulfills your wishes.
You can have joy
    even when ironing a load.
It's not something exciting
    if the truth be told.
You can have joy
    even when cleaning the commode.
It really doesn't have to be
    so great a woe.
You can have joy
    even when mowing the grass.
I know doing it with a push mower
    is no easy task.
You can have joy
    even when you've had a hard day at work.
You say that I really don't know
    just how much your head hurts.
You can have joy
    even when your child broke your vase.
You say please tell me how
    so, not to act in haste.
You can have joy
    even when reading this poem of mine.
Though it may bring back some memories
    that aren't so fine.
You can have *true* joy
    if Jesus is living through you.
What a change in attitude and perspective
    which He will do.

Jesus Said

(Matt 5:39, 44; 10:37-39; 11:29-30; Mark 9:23; Luke 9:23
John 14:2-3, 6; Acts 20:35)

Jesus said it is more blessed
>to give than to receive.
You must remind yourself every day
>for this to believe.
Jesus said you are to love your enemies
>and turn the other cheek.
You must totally depend on Christ's love,
>and for this you must seek.
Jesus said you are to deny yourselves
>and take up your own cross.
You must realize you will gain more
>than ever could be lost.
Jesus said to love Him more
>rather than you love things or family.
You can't do this without
>getting to know Him so intimately.
Jesus said no man can come to the Father
>except he come through the Son.
There's no other way to get to heaven,
>but only through Christ you must come.
Jesus said take His yoke and burden upon you,
>and it will be easy and light.
If you will only do so
>it will be for you such great delight.
Jesus said if you truly believe,
>you will be able to do amazing things.
He really wants you to know
>what trust and faith in Him will bring.

Our Savior's Birth

(A Christmas Hymn or Song)
(Matt 2:1-2, 11; Luke 2:7-18; 1 Corinthians 15:3; Colossians 1:16)

We celebrate this day our Savior's dear birth
    when born through a virgin came to this earth.
Oh what great love the Father did show.
    The greatest gift to receive He had bestowed.

The shepherds were the first to behold this wondrous sight:
    a baby wrapped in swaddling clothes on that first Christmas night.
The baby lying in a manger so very meek and mild
    would soon have wise men pre-sent gifts for this special child.

Hallelujah, sing His praises!
    Hallelujah, praise the Lord!
Hallelujah, sing His praises!
    Glorify Him forever, and evermore!

Little did they know, that He came to die for our sins
    so we'd have life through Him that would never end.
The Messiah had finally come, and it had long been awaited.
    This Child, that through Him, all things were created.

Christ who is the Lord of Lords and King and Kings.
    We this day rejoice and all our voices sing.
There is peace on earth and good will to all men
    in this precious gift wrapped in a baby which God did send.

Hallelujah, sing His praises!
    Hallelujah, Amen and Amen!
Hallelujah, sing His praises!
    Bless His name forever without end!

I Remember When

I have such fond memories of the days
  when I was young.
Life seemed much simpler then,
  and there were so many pleasures to choose from.
I remember there were no cell phones, iPhones,
  video games, internet, computers or cable TV.
But I remember all the boys played ball outside together,
  rode bicycles, played marbles, and climbed trees.
I remember the girls jumped rope, played jacks and hopscotch,
  listened to records, and only talked, not texted, on a phone.
I remember when gas was thirty cents a gallon,
  and eight thousand dollars could buy a nice home.
I remember going down to the creek
  and trying to catch crawdads in a cup.
I remember catching lightening bugs in a bottle
  and watching the bugs light up.
I remember camping in my own backyard
  in a tent under the light of a full moon.
I remember going to a movie theater for fifty cents
  and watching a double feature on Saturday afternoons.
I remember going to the lake to fish
  with just a worm dangling on a fishing pole.
I remember the smell of my granddad's outhouse
  when nature called and I had to go.
I remember when the milkman delivered
  jugs of milk to our house every week.
I remember waiting for the snow cone and ice cream trucks
  to come by that were such a treat.
I remember the homemade chocolate pies and cakes
  that Mom made that could not be matched.
I will never forget the mouthwatering biscuits
  and cornbread that my grandmother made from scratch.

I remember eating fresh from the garden:
  green beans, corn on the cob, okra and potatoes.
I remember eating a salad, many times, from our own onions,
  green peppers, cucumbers, lettuce, and tomatoes.
I remember we grew watermelons and cantaloupes
  that we enjoyed eating on hot summer days.
I remember my parents churning homemade ice cream
  that was so good words cannot convey.
I remember my dad teaching me how to write neatly
  and to learn my multiplication tables.
I remember my mom reading the Bible to me
  until I was older and more able.
I remember she taught me the importance to pray to God
  by having me kneel beside my bed each night.
I remember she taught me to obey the Lord
  and to always strive to do what is right.
And I remember when most people
  had a reverent respect and fear of the Lord.
I remember when most people went to church,
  and it was Jesus they wanted to live for.
I remember churches would have revival services
  that would last about a week.
I remember people getting saved and desiring to serve the Lord,
  and for His will and purpose only to seek.
I remember when our country was morally good,
  people honored the truth, and that distrust in authority was rare.
I remember when we could read the Bible in school,
  display the Ten Commandments and have teacher-led prayers.
Sadly, our nation today has greatly changed morally,
  and no longer can be considered a Christian nation.
We desperately need a Spirit-sent revival,
  a great spiritual awakening and a life-changing transformation.

Do Not Love the World
(1 John 2:15-17)

We are not to love the world
    or the things it contains.
If anyone loves the world,
    God's love in Him cannot remain.

For all that is in the world,
    the lusts and all its pride,
is not of the Father
    but is of the world where it resides.

The world is passing away
    and its lusts that it will not sever.
He who does the will of God
    shall abide with Him forever.

So don't get caught up in things
    that shall have no eternal worth.
Lay up treasures in heaven,
    and don't lay up treasures on earth.

This life cannot compare
    to the life that is to come.
A life that will forever be
    with God and God's Son.

Are you holding on to some things
    that are of this earth?
Let go of them today!
    They have no eternal worth!

For Whosoever Will

(John 3:16; Romans 10:9; 1 John 1:9; 1 John 3:1)

What manner of love
    the Father has bestowed so graciously
that we might become
    a child and a part of God's family.
For God so loved the world
    that included us, you see.
He gave His only begotten Son
    to whosoever shall believe.
Therefore, we don't have to face eternal death
    after this earthly life ends.
We can receive eternal life
    and a hope that only God can send.
If we will confess with our mouth
    that Jesus be our Lord.
If we will believe in our heart
    that God has raised Him to life evermore.
If we will confess our sins
    and are ready to repent.
God will forgive us through the cross
    where His Son He had sent.
Where Christ shed His blood
    to pay for the sins of mankind
so we can now see,
    and are no longer spiritually blind.
Praise the Lord! Praise the Lord!
    Praise Him with every breath!
Jesus will forgive all our sins
    so we can escape eternal death.
Praise the Lord! Praise the Lord!
    Praise Him and be still!
Jesus will gladly and forever save
    all the "whosoever" will.

God's Strength Made Perfect in Weakness
(1 Cor. 1:21; 2 Cor. 12:10)

The Bible says that God
    uses weak things to confound the wise.
It's from these weak things
    that God's strength and power are most realized.
The ordinary is able to do the extraordinary,
    and the weak are able to do more than the strong.
The less qualified become more than qualified,
    and God exalts those that are looked down upon.
The timid become very courageous,
    and the low-esteemed become confident and bold.
The ones that are forgotten and left out
    are now the ones that God graciously chose.
It's not that God doesn't use
    those strong, wise, and gifted,
but when He does, they are ones
    who must be surrendered, humble and sifted.
Jesus chose twelve men to teach and train
    that were the least likely to be taken.
When Jesus was beaten and crucified,
    He was left all alone and forsaken.
After Jesus was raised from the dead,
    these men were miraculously changed.
They were men, who turned the world upside down,
    and the world has never been the same.
When God works miracles through the weak,
    there is no question it's done through God's hand.
The weak are not capable on their own
    to accomplish the things that only God can.
Therefore it's important that we live our lives
    with humility, faith, and meekness.
Then, God's grace will be sufficient
    for His strength to be made perfect in our weakness.

Just for My Students

This poem is for those students who I did gladly teach
    in public and Christian schools and who I did try hard to reach.
I tried to impart to them math knowledge, facts and concepts;
    attempting to explain it so simply that they would never forget.
You must know that as important as math facts are
    they're not nearly as important as facts about God by far.
It is really our creator, who created, all true math.
    Man just discovers what God already created in the past.
The essence of numbers, are infinite like God, you see.
    What other subject can come close to explaining infinity?
Because God is infinite, He's hard for our minds to comprehend.
    But when revealed in His created acts, He's easier to believe in.
The square of the hypotenuse found in every right triangle
    equals the sum of its squared sides; formed by its right angle.
Pythagoras may have been credited with discovering this fact,
    but the areas he computed were by God's created act.
When every circle's circumference is divided by its diameter,
    you get the number pi that comes through God's parameters.
All of these are part of God's marvelous and created designs.
    This is just a sample of the wisdom that comes from God's mind.
That God would send His Son to give us eternal life,
    can easily be received by placing your faith in Jesus Christ.
In Christ you have all that God, so desires for you.
    Just believe and trust Him for all He wants to do.
This poem is as meaningful as any poem I've conceived.
    My hope is for a former student to believe and receive.
God can be trusted and believed in for sure.
    Through His Son you will find the strength to always endure.

There Is Eternal Hope
1 (Thessalonians 4:16-17; Revelation 21:4)

Does the world have you discouraged?
    Does it have you depressed?
Do shootings, viruses, wars, and inflation
    give you no rest?
Does it seem that this world
    will never get any better?
And does it mean that it will be
    like this forever?
God's Word predicted such bad things
    would happen in the last days.
And as you approach the end,
    you can expect goodness to crumble away.
So what hope do you have
    and will you be able to endure?
Is there any encouragement or joy
    that for you can be assured?
YES! There is comforting news
    that is found in God's Word.
Jesus shall rapture the saved to Heaven
    where you could have a place reserved.
He's prepared an eternal home
    where there will be no more sorrow.
A place called Heaven
    where there's no worry about a tomorrow.
You can have a peace and joy
    which in Heaven will never end.
You can experience a life of fulfillment,
    which on earth had never been.
In heaven there will be no more death,
    nor sorrow, nor crying.

You will be joyfully worshiping our Lord,
    and in Him forever abiding.
But you must repent of your sins
    and accept Christ's gift of salvation.
You must make Jesus your Lord
    so you can join in on the celebration.
Then you too will have this peace and joy
    to experience forever;
Enjoying in Heaven a life of fulfillment
    with God's family together.

Running Life's Race
(Matt. 25:23; 1 Cor. 9:24-26; 2 Timothy 4:7; Heb. 12:1)

There is a race in our life
  which we must all run.
It is one with many hills and deep valleys
  that are sure to come.
There will also be trials, tribulations
  and failures along the way.
It will take much strength
  and perseverance every single day.
The Bible tells us
  that those who run in a race, all run.
But only "one" receives the prize
  when the race is done.
We are to run so that the goal
  of victory will be met.
We will receive a crown,
  an imperishable one, we've longed to get.
We must lay aside every weight
  and the sin that besets each of us.
We are to run this race with courage
  and endurance which is a must.
We must look to Jesus,
  the author and the finisher of our faith:
A faith which gives us the strength
  to run well life's challenging race.
In the end Paul had fought the good fight
  and finished the race.
He had kept the faith
  and was now ready for Jesus to face.
The real prize that he desired
  was to hear words from God's Son:
For Jesus to say to him,
  "Thy good and faithful servant, WELL DONE!"

Let God Use You

The high school girl had just had a baby
    and was required to stay at home for a while.
A teacher would be needed to take assignments to her
    as she took care of her child.
A math teacher was found
    that volunteered to undertake this task.
He knew very well what was expected
    and the commitment that would be asked.
He went after school each day
    to deliver school assignments that she needed.
She would then give him the previous assignments
    that she had just completed.
He decided to do more
    than he had been requested to do.
He began tutoring her, mostly in math,
    so she would not fall behind in school.
So very often he would hold her child
    so she could take a test.
Sometimes he fed it with a bottle
    as he held the baby close to his chest.
She worked hard to complete all her work,
    and she passed for the year.
The teacher was so proud of her
    and couldn't help but shed a tear.
Without his help
    she might have dropped out of school.
She later became a teacher herself
    showing the same compassion for her students too.
We should always look for ways to help others
    and allow God to use us as He would choose.
We never know what influence we might have
    when we are willing for God to use.

The Resurrection and the Life
(John 11:25-26)

Jesus told us that He was
    the resurrection and the life.
He said if anyone believes in Him
    that they would *never* die.
What did Jesus mean by making
    such a bold statement?
It's that he'd win the victory over death
    soon by His coming sacrificial payment.

So when He suffered and died
    on a cross at Calvary,
Jesus shed His blood to atone
    for our sins most unselfishly.
He won a victory
    that we ourselves could never gain.
Praise the Lord for a sacrifice
    that was not given in vain.

We now have a hope
    and a glorious future with Christ.
We have a home made in Heaven
    prepared for our eternal life.
So we should never worry
    or ever be in doubt.
Our future is assured,
    and there's nothing to fear about.

His Name Is Jesus

(A Song or Hymn)

Does your life have purpose? Does it have real meaning?
    Have you found in your life something worth believing?
There *Is* good news, just for you, if you'll just believe;
    A hope, a joy, and a peace, that you can now receive.

There is one who died for you if you can only see.
    He gave His life to give you life, ever eternally.
His name is Jesus, and He offers you a gift that's totally free.
    But you, by faith, must take it; and that's the very key.

His name is Jesus! He gave His own life for you.
    His name is Jesus! He wants to abide in you.
His name is Jesus! He poured out His love for you.
    His name is Jesus! He died on the cross for you.

Be willing to let Him have your life each and every day;
    By trusting, abiding, and totally surrendered, ready to obey.
You can have real purpose and a Heavenly home.
    Jesus will be waiting beside His Father's throne.

Will you confess your sins and desire truly to repent?
    If you do, the Lord will hear and is ready to give His consent.
So you will be forgiven, pardoned, and made pure and free.
    You will become God's son, an heir, and part of God's family.

His name is Jesus! Just give your own life to Him.
    His name is Jesus! Just trust and abide in Him.
His name is Jesus! Just pour out your love for Him.
    His name is Jesus! Just die to oneself for Him.

This Is the Day
(Psalm 118:24; Lamentations 3:22-23; John 15:4; Phil. 4:6)

This is the day that the Lord hath made,
    and may I add,
we're to do our best to rejoice in it,
    and be glad.
The mercies of the Lord are new
    each and every morning.
For great is His faithfulness
    as each new day is dawning.
We're not to allow our yesterdays
    to affect each new day.
And we're also not to allow our tomorrows
    to cause worry or delay.
We must always live in the present
    enjoying life's journey.
We're to be excited about the day's possibilities
    and resting in God so firmly.
God has given us each day
    to be lived in His "rest."
We must choose to live it
    in a way He would bless.
We must live for Christ
    and not get in a big hurry,
and there is no better way
    but to try not to worry.
God's word tells us
    that in Christ we are to abide.
And in our Christian life
    we're not to struggle or strive.
So don't worry about things,
    especially those we can't control.
Worry only does us harm
    and causes us undo woe.

Cast Your Burdens upon the Lord
(Psalm 55:22)

Are you at this time
    going through a great burden?
And are you able to deal
    with so much hurtin'?
Do you feel you're unable,
    to keep pressing on,
and that any relief or answers
    seem all but gone?
God's Word tells you to cast
    all your burdens upon the Lord.
And if you do, the Lord will sustain
    and strengthen you all the more.
God's Word says He will never suffer
    the righteous to be moved,
but will begin the process
    for you to be healed and soothed.
The key is you must believe
    that God will carry you through.
He will give you the strength
    and the faith that it takes too.
If you are patient
    and persevere all the way to the end,
God will do a great work for you
    on which you can certainly depend.
There is nothing in your life
    that is too great for your Lord.
He is the Sovereign Creator,
    who by doubting you can't afford.
Whether in this life or the next,
    God will ease all your pain.
He'll take away this hurtin'
    and give you a joy you can't explain.

Two Years Ago, Today
(My mom passed away on December 22, 2019)

As I write this poem
    I'm thinking about the past.
Two years ago this very day
    my mom to Heaven did pass.
Though I miss her greatly
    and loved her with all my heart,
I know she's in a better place,
    and that comforts me while we're apart.
The pain she had suffered
    was so hard for me to cope.
So I placed her in the hands of God
    who gives me peace and hope.
She was prepared to go
    when it was to be God's time.
Mom had just turned eighty-eight,
    and was a long way from her prime.
God was so merciful
    and took her peacefully while sleeping.
My mom went to be with the Lord,
    and her soul was now in His safe keeping.
The assurance that she is in Heaven
    and in no more pain
gives me joy and peace while knowing
    I will see her once again.
I will always cherish our memories
    and the time we had together.
I do not grieve over her loss of life
    because she's in a place so much better.
You also may have lost a loved one,
    and it causes you much grief.

But God can give you what you need,
    much comfort and relief.
I hope you have the same assurance
    for your loved one as I do.
Just make sure that those
    who are still alive can say the same about you.
Remember, that receiving Christ
    as your Savior and Lord is the only way.
Then you can go to Heaven after you die,
    and there you will forever stay.
I made my decision for Christ
    years ago to accept His free gift.
I accepted His gift of salvation
    and the forgiveness of sin that it goes with.
I can't wait for that day
    when I will get to see my mom again.
What a glorious reunion it will be
    with my mom in *Glory-land*.

Pride

(Proverbs 16:18; Isaiah 64:8; 2 Cor. 5:15; James 4:6, 10)

There is always a danger
    when God gives us some ability to use,
to believe we accomplished everything
    by our own strength, which is not true.
Pride is the sin
    that caused the fall of mankind.
Pride is in all of us
    and it's so difficult to keep in line.
All our gifts and the abilities
    that we are able to do ourselves
were given to us by the Holy Spirit
    to use and do for God Himself.
We must constantly be on the alert
    so pride does not win out.
We must commit to be humble
    and live in a way so there's no doubt.
God's Word says that He "resists the proud
    but gives grace to the humble."
So it's important not to be proud
    and to make sure we don't stumble.
We are also to live for Christ
    and not for ourselves.
It's in Christ alone
    that all glory and honor must dwell.
So it's for Jesus we should desire
    to receive all the praise.
To praise Him for anything He does through us
    for the rest of our days.
We must fight daily
    so pride will not have its way.
We must always remind ourselves
    that "He's the potter and we are the clay."

Comfort Others as We Are Comforted
(2 Corinthians 1:4)

The young girl had just gone through
    many months of radiation treatments and chemo.
Her cancer was in remission,
    but if cured she could not know.
It had been a very long and painful ordeal
    that she had to go through.
But with the love and comfort of others,
    she was able to endure and make do.
She decided that she would like to share
    this same love and comfort for others.
So she encouraged other children going through cancer
    to help them sooner to recover.
She made it known throughout her town
    to donate stuffed animals and toys.
She knew that when given to these children with cancer
    would give them much hope and joy.
The town was excited to help,
    and stuffed animals and toys came flooding in.
She took them all to the children,
    and those items were such a "Godsend."
It made the girl feel happy
    that she could bring some joy to others in need.
Those who were hurting like she had
    were now able to have some of their pain relieved.
God expects us to truly care for others
    and to show them His comfort and love.
The comfort we're able to share
    only comes from God above.
Those that have experienced God's comfort
    are then able to give the same.
They are able to comfort others with the same comfort
    God gave them, a comfort in Jesus' name.

You Are Not Your Own
(John 10:10; 1 Corinthians 6:19-20; 2 Cor. 5:15)

If you are now a Christian
    and received eternal life,
your life is not your own,
    but it belongs to Jesus Christ.
Therefore you should no longer live your life
    just only for yourself.
Now you must live for Christ
    whose Spirit in you now dwells.
God's Word makes it clear
    that your body is the temple of Christ
Since His Spirit now resides in you,
    you should reflect Jesus in your life.
Jesus Christ has now purchased you
    at a tremendous price.
He died and shed His blood for you
    by giving His life at a great sacrifice.
It may be hard to comprehend
    just how much God loves you.
He loves you unconditionally
    even despite the bad things you do.
You can never repay the debt
    which you owe because of your sins.
Jesus took all your sins upon Himself
    so you can be forgiven and cleansed.
You can be assured
    that giving your life to Christ is no loss.
His plan and purpose He has for you
    is much greater than any cost.
He wants to give you a life
    more abundant than any you have known.
He will give you a life much greater
    than you could possibly live by yourself alone.

They Would Not Bow

(Daniel 3:8-30)

There is a story in the Bible where three Hebrew men
    refused to bow down to a king.
They knew that if they didn't bow,
    what the consequences of their refusal would bring.
They believed in the one true God
    and would not worship or serve any other.
They loved their God, and despite impending persecution,
    they would not bow down to another.
The day came for these three
    to be thrown into a raging furnace of fire.
Yet they stood bravely before this king
    and trusted completely on a power much higher.
They told the king that they would not bend,
    they would not bow, but would rather burn.
They testified that the God they serve was able
    to deliver them from this fire and give them a safe return.
But if their God chose not to do so,
    they would never serve other gods or idols
because their love and faith they had for their God
    was to them the most vital.
The king had them thrown into the fire,
    but what he saw he could not believe.
These three Hebrew men were untouched by the fire,
    and a fourth man in the fire he did see.
They were brought out of the furnace
    without the fire affecting them in any way.
The king then blessed the God of these three
    and made a decree that very day.
No one was to speak anything amiss
    about the one true God whose power was now affirmed.
Yes, these three Hebrew men did not bend,
    they did not bow, and miraculously they did not burn.

Spiritual Gifts
(Romans 12:6-8; 2 Corinthians 12: 4-11, 27-30)

God's Word says every Christian
    is given at least one gift or more.
But it's the Holy Spirit Who decides
    which person a gift is for.
We cannot ask or decide
    what gifts that we can choose.
It is out of our hands
    the gifts we're granted to use.
The Bible gives us a list of gifts
    for which we might yearn and long.
But they are to be used
    to help make the church be effective and strong.
So each gift mentioned below
    has been given to some person before,
and all the gifts have been given to
    at least one person or more.
God has given to some
    the gift to teach,
and to others
    He's given the gift to preach.
There's some that have been given
    the gift to encourage others.
He's also given
    the gift of helps to another.
He gives to a few
    a gift of exhibiting extraordinary faith.
God gives to many others
    a gift of showing uncommon grace.
There is also a gift from God
    to be used to sing.

To many He gives a gift
    to always have joy to bring.
He also has given to some
    the gift of hospitality.
He's given a gift to others
    the word of wisdom, gladly.
There are many more gifts
    which God to us does entrust.
But we must discover the gifts
    which He's given to us.
Is it possible for God
    to give another gift to one who is old?
Age does not matter when receiving a gift
    if the truth be told.
God's Word says the Holy Spirit
    always gives gifts as He wills.
So, who is to say to what person that
    another gift might be instilled.

Revival Finally Came

The pastor had recently been very discouraged
    because he had witnessed so little fruit.
He had prayed and prepared so diligently
    to preach urgently God's eternal truth.
Each Sunday, he hoped this might be the day
    that God would perform a great miracle.
He prayed the Church would experience revival
    where lives would be changed considerable.
Some people from the church had been praying a long time
    for God to bring a great revival.
They knew it was desperately needed
    even for the future of their church's own survival.
A few couldn't help but be a little discouraged,
    and doubt would occur even for some.
But the group determined they would never give up hope
    that revival was sure to come.
The pastor came to church that Sunday morning
    still discouraged, but with some hope.
He and the group had been praying fervently
    for God's Spirit to come down like a bolt.
The pastor had a strange feeling that morning
    as he began to enter the church's front door.
He felt something was about to happen
    that had never happened in this church before.
As they sang the hymns that morning,
    there was a strange and eerie feeling in the air.
People began to weep while singing,
    and for some it was more than they could bear.
Many began coming to the altar
    and kneeling down in desperate prayer.

Soon most of the church was down at the front,
    and they were all in much despair.
They were repenting of their sins
    and asking God to forgive them and show mercy.
God had clearly revealed to them
    that they were truly sinful and spiritually dirty.
Revival came gloriously upon them
    and filled the whole church that day.
Those that had been praying faithfully
    witnessed joyfully the power of God to have His way.

Temptations
(2 Corinthians 10:13; Hebrews 2:18, 4:15-16)

Is there some temptation
    which you are always giving in to?
Has it become a powerful addiction
    that is always controlling you?
You've desired to give it up,
    but it's something you can't do.
It's causing you such guilt and misery
    that you've continually gone through.
There is one who went through every temptation
    that you might possibly endure.
Since He never gave in to a temptation,
    He is now able to give you a cure.
Only Jesus can give you the strength and power
    that can set you free.
You must be willing to give up your life to Him,
    and you must do it completely.
The Bible says there is not a temptation
    that is unique just to you.
Other people have faced these same tempting desires,
    and there is not a temptation that is new.
Though it may seem impossible
    that this addiction can be overcome.
There is nothing impossible
    that can't be done through God's Son.
God will not suffer you to be tempted
    above what you are able to take.
He will give you His power to free you
    and lead you to victory for His sake.
He will help you and give you
    a way so these temptations you can bear.
So you can overcome the addiction
    with divine help and much prayer.

A New Heaven and a New Earth
(Revelation 21:1,4-6)

Now the first Heaven and the first Earth
    will pass away.
God is going to create new ones
    where we will forever stay.
He shall wipe away
    every tear from our eyes,
and there shall no longer be a reason
    for us to sorrow or cry.
God says there will never again
    be any more pain.
There will also be no more grief or sadness
    that will remain.
There will be no more death
    which anyone will go through.
We will live forever,
    and God will make all things new.
God proclaimed we can be assured
    that it will be done.
This is because it all comes through
    Jesus Christ, God's perfect Son.
God will give
    the fountain of water of life to all
who are written in the Book of Life
    and have answered the call.
Why would anyone not want to enjoy
    such happiness and peace?
Heaven will be so gloriously wonderful
    and it will never cease.
I cannot wait to experience
    what God has for me
when my time comes to leave this Earth
    for God's eternity.

The Unexpected Visitor

The old woman sat at home
    with nothing more to eat.
Her food cupboards were bare,
    and she just wanted to weep.
She was unable to get out
    and had lost all joy and hope.
She no longer had any perseverance
    and strength in which to cope.
She no longer had any family
    or friends to call upon.
She was so lonely
    and had very little faith to continue on.
Her house was run down
    and always so damp and cold.
Because of so little heat
    her house developed mildew and mold.
As she sat despondent,
    suddenly she heard a knock at the door.
She slowly rose and got up
    on legs, which were so feeble and sore.
When she opened the door
    she saw a man holding some bags.
She felt embarrassed for him to see her
    dressed in such rags.
He asked if he might
    give her some food and drink.
She was unable to say a word
    and didn't know what to think.
She asked him inside
    and if he would like to sit down in a chair.
He gave her his supplies
    and told her that he truly cared.

He told her his church
	could do much needed repairs for her home.
He saw that little had been done for it
	for so very long.
She was overwhelmed by his help
	and for his sincere concern.
She told him she was so grateful,
	but had no money to give in return.
He told her not to worry
	for everything would be done free.
He said his church would gladly help
	to meet all of her needs.
He talked with her awhile
	and prayed for her before leaving.
Her spirit now rose,
	and she had renewed hope for believing.
Whenever the Lord places someone
	on your heart to call or check upon,
obey God immediately
	and visit them soon or try to phone.
We must show God's love to others
	every chance that we get.
Because failing to do so
	could cause us much sorrow and regret.

To Please Our Father

When you were young,
     did you have a desire
to please your father
     whom you so admired?
You tried very hard
     so that he would be proud of you
by attempting to acquire his approval
     in everything you tried to do.
Wanting to please someone
     comes naturally for all of us.
We especially want to please those
     whom we so love and trust.
It hurts us to know we have disappointed
     those we love in some way.
It really hurts when it's a loved father
     whom we have failed to obey.
It should be no different
     for a Christian and his Lord.
We should have a desire to please God
     and be with Him in one accord.
We must want to show our love for Him
     in all we do or say.
We should obey Him completely
     and immediately without any delay.
We should love God our Father
     more than any other person or thing.
We should hunger for His presence daily
     and on Him only to cling.
Yes, to please our Heavenly Father
     should be our greatest desire.
There is no greater goal
     which we should strive for any higher.

The Boy and His King

The little boy sat playing in his sandbox
    with great imagination.
He built a mighty castle
    which would rule a great nation.
Its king was so mighty,
    and there was no greater one to be found.
No one could match his strength
    by any other king around.
He was a good and kind king
    who showed much compassion and care.
For a king to be so good and caring for his people
    was really something quite rare.
The boy loved his kingdom which
    in his mind he had created.
He sang and rejoiced
    and was so glad that he had made it.
When the boy became a young man
    he met a new Lord and King.
This King was greater, more loving
    and more worthy of esteem.
Jesus Christ was now the one
    he rejoiced in and praised.
Jesus redeemed his life,
    and he was now wonderfully saved.
He discovered Jesus loves him more
    than he could have possibly dreamed.
Jesus loved him so much more
    than even his childhood king.
Jesus was good, caring, loving, merciful,
    gracious, and kind.
Yes, there was no greater
    than anyone could ever find.

The Best Gift!

All the children were seated excitedly
    on the ground next to a church.
They were all waiting to open their shoebox of gifts
    delivered by Samaritan's Purse.
A homeless orphan child was among this group,
    also waiting to open his box.
He had recently been wandering the streets
    without any shoes or any socks.
As the children were given the signal
    to open their newly given gifts,
the homeless boy opened his
    and his spirit and hope began to lift.
There were all kinds of good things
    that he found in his box to enjoy.
Though you would never guess what he saw
    that gave him the most joy.
It was not the pencils, pens,
    pencil sharpeners, or the erasers.
It was not the two notebooks
    that contained the writing paper.
It was not the crayons, coloring books,
    shirt, or even the needed socks.
It was not the train whistle, backpack
    or the cup found in the box.
It wasn't even the rubber ball
    or the small red racing car.
It was something to him
    that was greater by far.
It was a bright yellow washcloth
    and two bars of soap.
These were the items that gave him
    the most joy and hope.

Now he could wash his dirty body
    and finally be clean.
He could wash the sores on his feet
    and feel the relief it would bring.
He could now even wash
    his head and his hair.
It would feel so refreshing
    and take away even more of his despair.
Each night when he lay down,
    he slept with the washcloth to give him peace.
He clutched it close like a security blanket,
    and for him it would be impossible to release.
Soon after receiving the shoebox, he heard the Gospel
    and about the ultimate gift God had given.
The homeless boy accepted God's gift of salvation,
    and now began truly livin'.
He had received the greatest gift
    that anyone could ever receive.
He received the gift of Jesus
    and by faith in Him he now believed.
He was adopted into God's family,
    and was now a child of the King.
God had now truly "cleansed" him
    with the forgiveness that only God could bring.
But the story does not end here
    because there is more good news to tell.
One year later he was again adopted,
    but by a Christian family, and all would end well.

You Say—God Will

You say you need no help
   and you can do it all alone?
God will show you differently
   how much you are wrong.
You say you can do all things
   by your own power?
God will teach you that you need Him—
   a mighty strong tower.
You say you have no need
   to be saved or redeemed?
God will convict you of sin
   and lead you to believe.
You say that all you have and own
   is because of you?
God will show you it's all His
   and even your life too.
You say that you would like
   the faith to believe?
God will give you that faith
   which is just what you need.
You say you don't think
   God can forgive you of all your sin?
God will forgive every sin
   and give you direction on how to begin.
You say that you're now ready
   to receive forgiveness and His Son too?
God will gladly give you salvation,
   peace and joy, which is all for you.
You say you are now saved
   and experience a life most complete?
God has truly changed you,
   and there's nothing that's so sweet!

Blind but I See

As I was rushing to catch my plane
    so not to be late,
there was a young girl selling apples
    as I was nearing my gate.
I accidently bumped into her,
    and all her apples fell to the floor.
I told her I was so sorry,
    but had to hurry for a plane to board.
I began feeling guilty
    and looked back one last time.
I was surprised to see
    that this young girl was actually blind.
So as I neared the gate
    and prepared to board my flight,
I couldn't get my mind off this girl
    whom I did not treat right.
I realized I had to go back to help
    and to admit my shame.
Though I knew by doing so,
    I would have to miss my plane.
I returned and helped her gather the apples
    and to get her back on her feet.
She thanked me for my help
    and for being so caring and sweet.
She then gave me a Gospel tract
    and asked if she might pray.
She prayed God would give me safe travels
    and bless me for the rest of my day.
Later I read that tract
    and asked Christ to be my Savior and Lord.
I was the one, who had actually been blind,
    but could now see as never before.

The Long Dark Night

Every Christian will at least once
    experience a long dark night.
This dry season of faith will feel like
    we are separated from God's sight.
The joyful pleasures of worship and singing
    may no longer feel exciting.
The reading and studying of God's Word
    may now seem less inviting.
The prayers we lift up to God
    may seem that they are not being heard.
But God hears and is still there,
    He's just giving us a different Word.
He's teaching us that living the Christian life
    can't always be based on feelings;
Nor can it be lived just for His blessings
    or for things only appealing.
God wants us to learn to live
    totally for Him every day.
He wants us to learn to trust Him
    no matter what comes our way.
We must learn to accept the bad
    as well as we accept the good.
Our Christian life cannot be based
    on just wanting to feel as we should.
He sometimes has to temporarily "wean" us off
    even many very good things.
It's because our Christian life of late
    has been based only on what He brings.
God desires that we mature spiritually
    and become more like Christ.
He wants us to be able to love Him unconditionally
    throughout each day of our life.

To Be a Better Brother

The little boy had just listened
    to his favorite BBN children's radio show.
There was something he heard
    that would help him to spiritually grow.
He had heard a lesson on the importance
    of being loving and kind to others.
He realized how unloving and unkind
    he had been to his little brother.
He decided he would change his behavior
    by treating his brother much better.
He would be more available
    so they could spend more time together.
He wanted to become a better Christian example
    and a better role model.
Maybe now his little brother
    would have a good example in which to follow.
He wanted to tell the BBN station
    how the children's program had affected him.
So he called and told them
    of the changes he would now begin.
He told them how truly sorry he was
    that he had treated his brother so badly.
The radio station was very grateful for his call
    and appreciated it most gladly.
They later played this taped call
    to encourage others who daily tune in.
It would touch the hearts of all who would hear
    the message the station had sent.
We could learn a lesson ourselves
    from the testimony of this little boy.
Every day we live, we should show to others
    much kindness, compassion, and joy.

Have You Ever?

Have you ever wondered how a flower grows
    with the glory and beauty that it wonderfully bestows?
Thought or pondered how it came to be.
    Oh such an amazing glorious thing to see?

Have you ever climbed a mountain to its peak?
    Then, when you saw the view you could hardly speak?
Thought or pondered how it came to be.
    Oh such an amazing glorious thing to see?

Have you ever stopped to enjoy a beautiful fall day
    when all the trees changed colors in a marvelous way?
Thought or pondered how it came to be.
    Oh such an amazing glorious thing to see?

Have you ever watched a mountain stream as it flows,
    or seen a waterfall waltzing and dancing as it goes?
Thought or pondered how they came to be.
    Oh such amazing glorious things to see?

Have you ever looked up on a dark clear night
    and beheld such a wondrous and glorious sight?
Thought or pondered how it came to be.
    Oh such an amazing glorious thing to see?

Have you ever witnessed the miracle of birth?
    Is there a more miraculous happening in all the earth?!
Thought or pondered how it came to be.
    Oh such an amazing glorious thing to see?

Have you ever witnessed God's Spirit take a life and fill?
    There's nothing in this world which is ever so real.
Thought or pondered how it came to be.
    Oh such an amazing glorious thing to receive?

Have you ever felt a hunger for God as never before?
    You could not get enough but wanted so much more.
Thought or pondered how it came to be.
    Oh such an amazing glorious thing to receive?

Have you ever written a poem or composed a song,
    when you've NEVER been able to do it for so long?
Thought or pondered how it came to be.
    Oh such an amazing glorious thing to receive?

Oh how I've thought and pondered all of these.
    God's works are too mind-boggling to believe.
To think how all these things could come to be.
    What amazing things there are to see and receive!

Great Faith
(Matt. 8:8-13; Luke 7:1-10)

A Roman centurion had a beloved servant
    who was paralyzed and would soon die.
Along with being paralyzed he was
    experiencing much pain and suffering beside.
The centurion had heard about a healer
    who was performing amazing miracles in the land.
This man had healed the deaf, the blind,
    the demon possessed, and also made the lame to stand.
The centurion truly believed that this healer
    could completely make his servant well.
So he left his house and went to find this healer
    named Jesus, and where He might dwell.
He heard that Jesus was in Capernaum and that
    great multitudes were following Jesus as He went.
Jesus had just healed a leper and had earlier
    preached a message for sinners to repent.
The centurion approached Jesus and pleaded
    for Him to heal his servant whom he dearly cared for.
Jesus said he would come to his house to heal his servant,
    and the centurion could not thank Him more.
The centurion humbly said that he was not worthy
    for Jesus to enter his home.
Then with tremendous faith he asked Jesus
    if He would just speak the word and only that alone.
Jesus told the crowd that He had not found
    such great faith even among the Jews.
Jesus then told him to go his way and said,
    "As you have believed, it will be done for you."
When the centurion returned home, he discovered
    his servant had been healed that very hour.
Jesus will honor our faith when we believe in Him
    and is always willing to grant to us His mighty power.

You Must Go to Jesus

(Matt. 9:18-22; Mark 5:25-34; Luke 8:43-48)

A woman had been suffering from a hemorrhage
    that no one was able to cure for twelve years.
She had spent all the money she possessed
    and for years she had cried many tears.
She heard about a man called Jesus
    that was doing miraculous feats.
She believed if she could only go to Him
    her problem could finally be beat.
But a woman with her problem
    might be harshly treated by the crowd.
She wondered when she approached Jesus
    if she should speak His name out loud.
Jesus happened to be on His way
    to raise a ruler's daughter from the dead.
The woman quickly fought through the crowd
    and saw Jesus just ahead.
The moment had now come, but the woman
    wasn't sure what she should do.
How could, she get Jesus' attention
    without bringing attention to her too?
She believed that just by touching
    the hem of His garment that she would be healed.
So she reached out and touched His hem
    believing her desire would be fulfilled.
Jesus then turned to ask who had touched Him,
    and who desired for His healing to seek.
The woman now realized she could not hide
    and fell down trembling at Jesus' feet.
She declared why she did it and believed she was healed
    because her hemorrhaging had just now ceased.
Jesus told her to be of good cheer, that her faith
    had made her whole, and that she should go in peace.

The Teacher

There were many students
    the teacher had taught in a math class
that had no confidence
    because of bad experiences in their past.
Many had never enjoyed much success
    in their math classes before.
Some were told they were too dumb,
    and this contributed to their low scores.
He discovered with much encouragement
    and a belief they could succeed
that the students slowly began to improve
    and to believe they could achieve.
Many had been weak on basic fundamentals
    that needed to be improved.
Some just needed more confidence
    in their ability of what they could do.
The teacher encouraged them to ask questions
    and told them no question was dumb.
He worked hard to convince them
    that math could actually be fun.
He tried to always be positive,
    and wanted them to think that way too.
He encouraged them to develop good work habits
    and give their best in all that they do.
It was always an enjoyable challenge
    to teach math as simply as he could,
and break down difficult math concepts
    so they could be easily understood.
The teacher showed how each new math skill
    would build on one another;
So learning each previous one
    was the key for learning all others.

He realized not every math student
    learned math the exact same way.
So he taught using different ways and methods
    that helped many to get better grades.
He had many students who previously hated math
    that now liked it a lot more.
This made the teacher's teaching experience
    a truly enjoyable and meaningful reward.
The teacher learned early on
    that he could achieve nothing without the Lord.
Only God could give him the wisdom and patience
    that every day he had to pray for.

The One I Will Live For

(First Ever Poem)
(A Song or Hymn)

Ever since that wonderful day, that I received my new birth.
    I'm living each day as if my last faithfully on this earth.
I shall live my life in the light and glory of eternity
    until I go to my heavenly home where I will forever be.

I sincerely desire to surrender my life
    to my precious Savior and Lord who is Jesus Christ.
I also desire to abide in Him and to have Christ abide in me.
    This is my prayer and hope and my sincere plea.

Jesus glorious Jesus, I praise you, my Lord.
    Jesus wonderful Jesus, the One I truly adore.
Jesus merciful Jesus, I will praise you ever more.
    Jesus gracious Jesus, the One I will live for.

My body is the Lord's temple and He will forever live in me.
    I must take good care of it and let God make it ho-ly.
If my mind is to become, so much like the mind of Christ,
    I must guard and protect it from temptation and the world's vice.

Jesus loves me even more than I could possibly ever know.
    So I have peace and joy wherever I go.
My soul hungers and thirsts for my dear wonderful Lord.
    He's the one I will always desire to show my love for.

Jesus glorious Jesus, I praise you, my Lord.
    Jesus wonderful Jesus, the One I truly adore.
Jesus merciful Jesus, I will praise you ever more.
    Jesus gracious Jesus, the One I will live for.

www.ingramcontent.com/pod-product-compliance
Lightning Source LLC
Chambersburg PA
CBHW051006050726
47592CB00007B/2733